The Big Ideas Club Presents

Young Minds Living Philosophy

Plato's Timaeus for Kids

By Jason Kassel

© 2026

Recursive Publishing

Parents and Caregivers

This chapter was written for children—but not only for children.

It was written for reading together.

Plato believed that philosophy does not begin with answers. It begins with attention: noticing what holds, what moves, and what belongs together. That is a habit children already have, long before they learn names for it. What they often lack is permission to stay with hard ideas without being rushed to conclusions.

This series is meant to offer that permission.

What this chapter is (and is not)

This is not a simplified textbook.

It is not a moral lesson disguised as a story.

And it is not meant to explain everything.

Instead, it is a guided walk through ideas, shaped the way Plato himself thought: slowly, carefully, and out loud.

In these pages, Plato is imagined walking a circular path, speaking his thoughts as they form. An unnamed scribe walks beside him, trying—sometimes struggling—to write them down. Nearby, three children sit beneath an olive tree. They hear only fragments of what is said. They misunderstand. They argue. They wait.

This is intentional.

Plato did not believe that understanding arrives all at once. He believed it grows through return.

How to read this book

You do not need to read every page in one sitting. In fact, it works better if you don't.

Each chapter in this series is about 3,000 words—long enough to carry one idea, short enough to pause without losing it. You might read a few pages at a time, or a whole section in one evening, then stop.

The questions at the end of each chapter are not quizzes. There are no right answers hidden inside them. They are invitations to talk, wonder, and sometimes to sit quietly together without resolving anything.

If a child asks a question you can't answer, that is not a problem. Plato would have thought it was a good sign.

Why the structure matters

You may notice that ideas repeat across the books, returning in slightly different ways. This is not redundancy. It is the point.

Plato believed that many things come in pairs—fast and slow, same and different, desire and understanding—but that pairs alone do not hold together. Something must stand between them. A middle. A measure. A way of holding without forcing.

This idea appears again and again because it appears again and again in life.

Children recognize this instinctively. Adults often forget it.

Your role as a reader

You are not expected to teach philosophy here. You are invited to model curiosity.

If you pause when the scribe pauses, if you laugh lightly when writing feels hard, if you admit that some things take time to understand, you are already doing exactly what this chapter asks.

Reading together is not about mastering ideas. It is about showing that thinking is something people do with one another.

A final reassurance

Some parts of this chapter may feel quiet. Some may feel abstract. That does not mean children are missing something. It often means they are listening.

Plato trusted that understanding grows when it is not rushed.

So take the walk at your own pace.

Return when you need to.

And don't worry if you're not sure how to finish.

As the scribe learns, not knowing yet is often the clearest sign that thinking has begun.

Why the World Is Ordered

Letter to the Reader

Before we ask how to live, we must ask a quieter question.

We must ask what kind of world we live in at all.

Some people begin by asking what rules they should follow, or what choices are right or wrong. Plato did not begin there. He believed that questions about life come too late if we have not first wondered whether the world itself makes sense.

If the world were only an accident—if things simply happened and fell apart again—then asking how to live well would be like asking how to build a house on sand. But if the world has order, if things belong together for a reason, then learning to live is really learning to listen.

The account you are about to read was not written all at once. It was spoken, slowly, while walking. Some parts were clear right away. Others only made sense after returning to them again.

This chapter does not ask you to agree.

It asks you to walk beside an idea long enough to see whether it holds.

The First Circuit

Plato walked along the curved path with his hands clasped behind his back. The stones beneath his feet were smooth from years of passing steps, worn not down but into place.

Beside him walked a scribe, tablet tucked under one arm, stylus ready. The scribe had learned not to interrupt too quickly. Plato often spoke for several steps before the shape of a thought appeared.

"Most people," Plato said at last, "think the world is ordered because it follows rules."

The scribe scratched a mark. "Rules," he repeated.

Plato shook his head. "Rules explain how things behave once they exist. They do not explain why things belong together in the first place."

They passed a low olive tree standing slightly in from the path. Its branches reached outward, but its trunk leaned inward, as if listening.

"If you see a house standing," Plato continued, "you do not explain it by saying the stones obey gravity. You ask why the stones were placed together at all."

The scribe frowned. "So order comes before rules."

"Much before," Plato said. "And it comes from something simpler."

They walked in silence for a few steps.

"Goodness," Plato said.

The scribe stopped writing.

"Goodness?" he asked.

Plato kept walking.

The Spoken Account — First Pass

"When we say something is ordered," Plato said, "we usually mean it is not random. But that only tells us what it is not."

The scribe hurried to keep pace. "And what is it?"

Plato gestured outward, toward the path curving gently ahead of them. "Order means that parts relate. That one thing belongs with another. That difference does not pull everything apart."

"Like the two sides of the path," the scribe offered.

Plato smiled slightly. "Yes. But notice—two sides alone do not make a path. Something must hold them together."

The scribe looked down. Between the edges of stone lay packed earth, firm and walkable.

Plato slowed. "If the world had only extremes—only opposites—it would tear itself apart. Heat and cold. Fast and slow. Same and different."

The scribe wrote quickly. "Two sides are not enough."

"Exactly," Plato said. "Difference appears quickly. Unity is harder to keep."

They rounded the curve again. The olive tree came back into view.

The Spoken Account — Second Pass

"The Maker of the world," Plato said, "did not begin with chaos and force it into shape. He began with what is good."

The scribe hesitated. "Should I write 'Maker'?"

"Yes," Plato said. "But not as a craftsman who struggles. Write it as a reason that chooses."

"A choosing reason," the scribe murmured.

Plato nodded. "Goodness does not push. It draws things into fitting places."

They walked past the tree again, this time closer. Its roots disappeared into the soil from several directions, meeting beneath the ground.

"Between sameness and difference," Plato said, "there must be something else. Not a side. A middle."

The scribe paused, stylus hovering.

"So there are two... and then something between them."

Plato stopped walking.

"Yes," he said. "That is exactly where order begins."

The scribe exhaled.

"I am writing," he said, "but I don't yet know what I'm writing."

Plato smiled.

"Good. Then you're still thinking."

They resumed walking.

The Spoken Account — Third Pass

They had nearly completed the circle now. The path curved gently back toward where they had begun, though it did not feel like a return so much as a deepening.

"When the Maker chose what is good," Plato said, "he did not erase difference. He gave it a place."

The scribe nodded, writing more slowly now. "So difference isn't the problem."

"No," Plato said. "Difference without relation is."

They walked in silence for several steps.

"Think of a stretched string," Plato continued. "Pulled too tight, it snaps. Left slack, it makes no sound. Only when it is held between does it become music."

The scribe looked up. "So the middle doesn't weaken the pull. It makes it usable."

Plato's eyes brightened. "Yes. And what is usable can be shared."

They passed the olive tree once more. Its leaves rustled lightly, though there was no wind. Plato lowered his voice, not as if someone were listening, but as if the thought itself required care.

"The world is ordered," he said, "because something stands between its extremes. Not as a wall. As a bond."

The scribe hesitated again. "Bond... or harmony?"

Plato considered this. "Write harmony. Bonds can be forced. Harmony belongs."

The scribe wrote.

They slowed their pace. The path felt familiar now beneath their feet.

"So when people ask why the world holds together," Plato said, "they are really asking whether there is anything that keeps difference from becoming destruction."

"And your answer?" the scribe asked.

Plato did not stop walking.

"My answer," he said, "is that the world was made to belong."

They completed the circuit.

Between the Columns — Under the Olive Tree

Theo sat cross-legged beneath the olive tree, tracing shapes in the dust with a thin stick. Mira leaned back against the trunk, watching the light flicker through the leaves. Leo lay on his stomach, chin propped on his hands.

Plato and the other man passed again, their voices drifting closer, then farther.

"...not a side," Plato was saying. "A middle."

Theo looked up. "Did you hear that?"

Mira nodded. "He keeps saying it."

Leo frowned. "A middle of what?"

They fell quiet as the voices faded.

Theo tapped the stick against the ground. "Maybe it's like when two people are pulling on something, and it rips."

"And someone steps in," Mira said, "so it doesn't."

Leo rolled onto his back. "So the middle isn't boring. It's busy."

They listened again.

"...difference belongs," Plato's voice drifted back to them, then disappeared.

Theo smiled. "I think that's important."

Leo shrugged. "I think it's confusing."

Mira closed her eyes. "I think we'll hear it again."

The Last Circuit

Plato and the scribe continued walking, though the scribe no longer wrote every word.

"Some things," Plato said, "cannot be understood the first time they are heard."

The scribe nodded. "Or the second."

Plato glanced toward the olive tree, where the children sat quietly now, not listening so much as waiting.

"What matters," Plato said, "is not reaching the center."

"But returning near it," the scribe offered.

Plato smiled. "Exactly."

They walked on.

🫒 Under the Olive Tree — Let's Talk

- What do you think Plato means by a "middle"?

- Can you think of a time when two sides pulled apart and needed something between them?

- Why do you think Plato says goodness comes before rules?

- Is harmony something you can force, or something that has to fit?

- Why might returning to an idea help you understand it better?

Take your time. These questions are meant for walking, not rushing.

🧠 Learn Like Plato!

A word to notice:

 Good — not as a reward, but as what makes things belong together.

Try this thinking practice:

Look at something that works well—a team, a game, a routine, even a conversation.

Ask yourself:

- What are the two sides that could pull apart?

- What stands between them?

- What would happen if that middle disappeared?

You don't need to answer out loud.

Just notice.

That is how thinking begins.

The World as a Living Whole

Letter to the Reader

In the first chapter, Plato asked whether the world belongs together at all.

Now he asks something stranger.

If the world is ordered—if it holds together on purpose—then what kind of thing is it?

Most people think of the world as a place filled with things. Stones. Trees. Animals. People. Stars. Plato asked whether this way of seeing misses something more important.

What if the world is not just a collection?

What if it is a whole?

This chapter does not ask you to imagine the world as alive in the way an animal is alive. It asks you to imagine life more carefully than that.

The First Circuit

Plato walked more slowly today. His steps followed the curve of the path almost exactly, as if he were testing whether it would hold him.

The scribe walked beside him, tablet ready, stylus already stained with ink.

"You wrote yesterday," Plato said, "that order requires a middle."

"Yes," the scribe replied. "Though I'm not sure I understood it."

Plato nodded. "Good. Today, you will see what stands in that place."

They passed the olive tree. Its branches reached outward unevenly, yet the whole tree leaned together, balanced.

"Most people," Plato said, "think life means breathing."

The scribe hesitated. "Doesn't it?"

"It is a sign," Plato replied. "Not a definition."

They continued walking.

"Life," Plato said, "is what moves itself in an ordered way."

The scribe wrote quickly. "Moves itself... but doesn't fall apart."

Plato smiled faintly. "Now you're listening."

The Spoken Account — First Pass

"If the world were only built," Plato said, "it would be stiff. If it were only moving, it would scatter."

The scribe frowned. "So it must be both."

"Yes," Plato said. "But not separately."

They walked past the tree again.

"The Maker did not place soul into the world," Plato said. "He formed the world with soul."

The scribe slowed. "You mean the world has a soul."

Plato raised one finger—not to correct, but to steady the thought.

"Not like yours," he said. "Not with fear or desire. But with motion, proportion, and care."

They stopped briefly.

"Between sameness and difference," Plato continued, "the Maker wove something that could bind both."

The scribe looked up. "The middle again."

"Yes," Plato said. "But now it is alive."

The Spoken Account — Second Pass

"The soul of the world," Plato said, "was made from harmony itself."

The scribe blinked. "Harmony isn't a thing."

"Exactly," Plato replied. "It is a relation."

They walked on.

"When two notes are too close, they blur. When too far apart, they clash. Harmony belongs between."

The scribe scribbled, then paused. "So the soul isn't at the edge."

"No," Plato said. "It is what lets the edges belong."

They passed the olive tree again. The scribe noticed how its roots curved inward beneath the soil.

"The world moves," Plato said, "because its soul moves it—not by pushing, but by turning."

"Turning," the scribe repeated.

"In circles," Plato said. "Always returning, never collapsing."

The scribe stopped writing.

"I am writing," he said, "but I don't yet know what holds all of this together."

Plato smiled.

"Good. Then you're still thinking."

They resumed walking.

The Spoken Account — Third Pass

"The world," Plato said, "is one living thing."

The scribe finally said what he had been holding back.

"But it doesn't eat," he said. "It doesn't sleep."

Plato laughed softly. "Neither does a thought. And yet it lives."

They walked more slowly now.

"A living whole," Plato said, "does not mean every part feels. It means every part belongs."

The scribe nodded. "So nothing is wasted."

"Nothing is accidental," Plato corrected gently.

They passed the olive tree once more. A bird startled from its branches and flew upward, then curved back down to land again.

"The soul of the world," Plato said, "does not rule like a king. It holds like a rhythm."

The scribe wrote that down carefully.

"When people feel calm looking at the sky," Plato added, "it is because their own souls recognize the pattern."

They completed the circuit.

Between the Columns — Under the Olive Tree

Mira lay on her back beneath the olive tree, watching the leaves move against the sky.

Theo sat beside her, knees pulled up. Leo tossed a pebble into the dirt and watched it bounce.

"...a living whole," Plato's voice drifted past.

Theo whispered, "Did he say the world is alive?"

Leo scoffed. "It doesn't even blink."

Mira didn't answer right away.

"It doesn't have to," she said. "You can tell when something fits."

Theo smiled. "Like music."

Leo stopped tossing the pebble. "So if it's alive... does it listen?"

They fell quiet.

"...not at the edge," Plato's voice returned. "Between."

Mira closed her eyes. "I think the middle is doing most of the work."

The Last Circuit

Plato and the scribe walked on, the path now deeply familiar.

"Do not think," Plato said, "that calling the world alive makes it gentle."

The scribe raised an eyebrow. "It doesn't feel gentle."

"No," Plato said. "Life is not softness. It is order that moves."

The scribe nodded slowly.

"So the world holds together," he said, "because its soul keeps returning."

Plato smiled. "And because nothing is left outside."

They completed the circle again, and again slowed.

🌿 Under the Olive Tree — Let's Talk

- What do you think it means to call the world a "living whole"?

- Can something be alive without breathing or thinking like a person?

- Why might harmony be more important than strength?

- Where do you see patterns that make things belong together?

- How do you know when something fits—even if you can't explain why?

🧠 Learn Like Plato!

A word to notice:

Harmony — not as sameness, but as fitting difference together.

Try this thinking practice:

Listen closely to something with rhythm—music, footsteps, waves, or even your own breathing.

Ask yourself:

- What are the different parts?

- What keeps them from clashing?

- What would happen if the middle were missing?

You don't need to answer.

Just notice how belonging sounds.

Time and the Stars

Letter to the Reader

By now, Plato has said something surprising.

He has said the world belongs together.

He has said it is a living whole.

But there is a problem that follows immediately.

If the world is ordered and alive, why does it change?

Why does everything move, grow old, return, and pass away?

This chapter does not try to stop time.

It asks what time is for.

The First Circuit

The path felt different today.

Not narrower or wider, but measured—each step seeming to answer the last. Plato walked with his eyes lifted more often now, glancing upward between sentences.

The scribe noticed and adjusted his pace.

"You are looking at the sky," he said.

Plato nodded. "Because what we are about to speak of cannot be understood by standing still."

They passed the olive tree. Its shadow had shifted since yesterday, stretching farther across the path.

"People think time is obvious," Plato said. "They say it passes."

The scribe scratched a mark. "Doesn't it?"

Plato smiled. "That is what it seems to do. But seeming is not the same as being."

They continued walking.

"Before the world moved," Plato said, "there was no time."

The scribe stopped short. "Then what was there?"

Plato did not stop walking.

The Spoken Account — First Pass

"There is something," Plato said, "that does not change."

The scribe hurried to keep up. "Something outside time."

"Yes," Plato replied. "Not outside as in far away. Outside as in untouched."

They rounded the curve.

"This," Plato continued, "is what we call eternity. Not endless days. Not forever waiting. But complete presence."

The scribe frowned. "Then time is... less?"

Plato shook his head. "Different."

They passed the olive tree again.

"If eternity stayed alone," Plato said, "it could not be seen. If change moved alone, it would never return."

The scribe looked down at his tablet. "Two sides again."

"Yes," Plato said. "And again, not enough."

The Spoken Account — Second Pass

"Time," Plato said, "was made when the heavens were set in motion."

The scribe looked up sharply. "Made?"

"Yes," Plato said. "As a companion."

They walked beneath a break in the trees. The sky opened above them.

"The stars," Plato said, "were placed so that motion could be counted."

"Counted?" the scribe echoed.

"So that change could belong to order," Plato replied. They walked on.

"Time is not the opposite of eternity," Plato said. "It is its image."

The scribe paused his writing. "An image that moves."

Plato nodded. "Always moving. Always returning."

They passed the olive tree once more. Its shadow crossed the path like a slow hand sweeping a circle.

"I am writing," the scribe said, "but it keeps moving while I do."

Plato smiled.

"Good. Then you're still thinking."

The Spoken Account — Third Pass

"Notice," Plato said, "that time does not rush."

The scribe raised an eyebrow. "It feels like it does."

"That is because you are inside it," Plato replied. "From within, motion feels like pressure."

They slowed their pace.

"Time," Plato said, "stands between what never changes and what never stops changing."

The scribe nodded slowly. "The middle again."

"Yes," Plato said. "But now it is measure."

They walked in silence for several steps.

"When people watch the sky," Plato said softly, "they learn patience without being taught."

The scribe wrote that down.

"Time teaches the soul," Plato continued, "by return."

They completed the circuit.

Between the Columns — Under the Olive Tree

Theo lay on his back beneath the olive tree, counting something only he could see.

"Three... four... five..."

Mira sat nearby, watching the shadows move across the ground. Leo kicked at the dirt with his heel.

"...an image," Plato's voice drifted toward them.

Theo sat up. "Did he say time is a picture?"

Leo snorted. "Pictures don't move."

Mira shaded her eyes. "Maybe it's a picture you walk through."

Theo smiled. "That would explain why it takes so long."

They listened again.

"...always returning," the voice said, then faded.

Leo frowned. "If it keeps coming back, why does it feel like it's going away?"

Mira answered quietly. "Maybe because we're the ones moving."

The Last Circuit

Plato and the scribe walked more slowly now. The light had shifted again, and the sky was deeper in color.

"Time is not a mistake," Plato said. "Nor a punishment."

The scribe nodded. "It's a helper."

"Yes," Plato replied. "A middle that lets change belong to what lasts."

They passed the olive tree once more.

"Without time," Plato said, "nothing could be learned."

The scribe closed his tablet gently.

They continued walking.

🫒 Under the Olive Tree — Let's Talk

- What do you think Plato means by eternity?

- How is time different from just "things passing"?

- Why might time need to return in patterns?

- Do you think time teaches us something? What?

- How does it feel to wait, remember, or notice change?

🫒 Learn Like Plato!

A word to notice:

Time — not as a clock, but as measured motion.

Try this thinking practice:

Watch something that moves in a pattern—a shadow, a swing, the sky, or your breathing.

Ask yourself:

- What stays the same?

- What changes?

- What lets them belong together?

You don't need to answer.

Just notice the rhythm.

The Human Soul

Letter to the Reader

Up to now, Plato has looked outward.

He has spoken of the world, of harmony, of time, and

of the slow order of the stars. But there is a question

that waits quietly behind all of this.

If the world is so carefully held together,

 why do we feel pulled apart?

This chapter turns inward—not to judge, but to

notice.

The First Circuit

Plato walked more slowly today, as if listening for

something that did not make noise.

The scribe matched his pace without being asked.

"You have spoken of the world's soul," the scribe

said. "And of time as its measure."

Plato nodded.

"But people," the scribe continued, "do not feel like living wholes."

Plato stopped walking.

"No," he said. "They feel like crossings."

They resumed the circle.

The Spoken Account — First Pass

"The human soul," Plato said, "was made from the same pattern as the world's."

The scribe raised his eyes. "Then why does it feel so different?"

Plato smiled gently. "Because it is placed inside a body."

They passed the olive tree. Its bark was rougher here, scarred by time and weather.

"The soul," Plato said, "belongs to order. The body belongs to change."

The scribe wrote. "Two sides again."

"Yes," Plato said. "And again, not enough."

They continued walking.

"When the soul forgets its measure," Plato said, "it is pulled apart."

The scribe frowned. "By what?"

"By wanting without seeing," Plato replied. "And by seeing without care."

The Spoken Account — Second Pass

"The soul," Plato said, "is not broken by having many parts."

The scribe looked up. "Then why does it feel broken?"

"Because its parts do not listen to one another," Plato replied.

They passed the olive tree again.

"Reason," Plato said, "does not rule by force."

The scribe paused. "Then how does it rule?"

"By standing between," Plato said. "By hearing both sides."

The scribe wrote more slowly now.

"When desire pulls," Plato continued, "and understanding hesitates, something must hold."

The scribe nodded. "The middle again."

Plato smiled. "Always."

"I am writing," the scribe said quietly, "but this feels harder than the others."

Plato glanced at him.

"Good. Then you're still thinking."

They walked on.

The Spoken Account — Third Pass

"The soul," Plato said, "was meant to be tuned."

The scribe tilted his head. "Like a string?"

"Yes," Plato said. "Or a voice."

They slowed their pace.

"When the soul listens only to desire," Plato said, "it becomes loud but empty."

"And when it listens only to rules?" the scribe asked.

"It becomes silent," Plato replied. "And brittle."

They passed the olive tree once more. A breeze moved the leaves unevenly, then settled.

"The soul holds together," Plato said, "when reason stands between what pulls and what knows."

The scribe wrote that down carefully.

"This is why learning is not filling," Plato added. "It is remembering how to listen."

They completed the circuit.

Between the Columns — Under the Olive Tree

Leo sat with his back against the trunk, arms crossed.

"I don't like it," he said.

Theo looked up. "What?"

"All this talk about being pulled apart," Leo replied.

"It feels true."

Mira traced the edge of a leaf with her finger.

"...stands between," Plato's voice drifted past.

Theo whispered, "Maybe that's why thinking is tiring."

Leo scowled. "Then why bother?"

Mira answered softly. "Because it's what keeps you together."

They fell silent as the voices moved away.

The Last Circuit

Plato and the scribe walked on, the path now deeply worn beneath their feet.

"Do not mistake struggle for failure," Plato said.

The scribe nodded. "It feels like falling apart."

"Sometimes," Plato replied, "it is learning to hold."

They passed the olive tree once more.

"The soul is not meant to be still," Plato said. "It is meant to be aligned."

The scribe closed his tablet gently.

They continued walking.

🫒 Under the Olive Tree — Let's Talk

- Why do you think Plato says the soul feels pulled apart?

- What does it mean for reason to "stand between" desire and understanding?

- Have you ever felt louder but emptier? Or quieter but brittle?

- Why might learning be more like remembering than collecting facts?

- What helps you feel whole again?

🧠 Learn Like Plato!

A word to notice:

Reason — not as control, but as listening.

Try this thinking practice:

The next time you feel pulled in two directions, pause.

Ask yourself:

- What is pulling?

- What is warning?

- What might stand between them?

You don't need to decide right away.

Just notice the space where holding happens.

Living in Harmony

Letter to the Reader

Across these books, Plato has asked large questions.

He has asked whether the world belongs together.

He has asked how time helps order appear.

He has asked why the human soul feels pulled apart.

Now he asks the hardest question of all.

If the world is held together by harmony,

and if the soul is meant to be tuned,

then how should a person live?

This book does not offer rules.

It offers a way of holding.

The First Circuit

Plato walked with an ease the scribe had not seen before.

Not because the thoughts were simple, but because they had been returned to many times.

"You have spoken of the soul," the scribe said. "And of reason as what stands between."

Plato nodded.

"But people want instructions," the scribe continued. "They want to know what to do."

Plato smiled. "Then they are asking too late."

They passed the olive tree. The children were there again, quieter now, as if listening had become familiar.

"Living well," Plato said, "is not a list of actions."

The scribe frowned slightly. "Then what is it?"

Plato did not answer immediately.

The Spoken Account — First Pass

"Consider the body," Plato said. "It is neither enemy nor master."

The scribe wrote. "A partner."

"Yes," Plato said. "But an uneven one."

They walked on.

"When the body is ignored," Plato said, "it weakens the soul. When it is indulged, it drowns it."

The scribe looked up. "Two sides again."

"And again," Plato said, "not enough."

They passed the olive tree once more.

"Health," Plato said, "is not strength. It is balance."

The scribe paused. "So living well is... staying in the middle."

Plato nodded. "But not by standing still."

The Spoken Account — Second Pass

"Measure," Plato said, "is what allows movement without collapse."

The scribe wrote carefully. "Measure."

"It is not less," Plato continued. "It is fitting."

They walked more slowly now.

"When people seek pleasure alone," Plato said, "their lives grow loud and thin."

"And when they seek order alone?" the scribe asked.

"They grow quiet and brittle," Plato replied.

They passed the olive tree again. The children were no longer speaking.

"To live in harmony," Plato said, "is to let each part have its voice without letting any part rule alone."

The scribe hesitated.

"I am writing," he said, "but I don't yet know where a life ends."

Plato smiled.

"Good. Then you're still thinking."

The Spoken Account — Third Pass

"Philosophy," Plato said, "is not separate from living."

The scribe looked surprised. "People think it is."

"That is because they think thinking is apart from motion," Plato replied.

They walked on.

"A well-lived life," Plato said, "is one that listens."

"To what?" the scribe asked.

"To the world," Plato said. "To the soul. And to the space between them."

They slowed their pace.

"Wisdom," Plato said, "is not knowing what to choose."

"It is knowing how to hold," the scribe finished.

Plato nodded.

They completed the circuit.

Between the Columns — Under the Olive Tree

Theo leaned against the trunk, eyes half-closed.

"He keeps talking about balance," he said.

Leo kicked at the dirt. "That sounds like work."

Mira watched a leaf fall, spin, and land.

"...not standing still," Plato's voice drifted past.

Theo opened one eye. "Maybe balance moves."

Leo frowned. "That sounds harder."

Mira smiled. "But it doesn't tear."

They listened as the voices faded.

The Last Circuit

Plato and the scribe walked one final time around the path.

"Do not expect harmony to feel perfect," Plato said.

The scribe nodded. "It feels fragile."

"Yes," Plato replied. "Because it must be renewed."

They passed the olive tree once more.

"Living well," Plato said, "is not reaching the middle once."

"It's returning to it," the scribe said.

Plato smiled.

They walked on.

🫒 Under the Olive Tree — Let's Talk

- What do you think it means to live in balance?

- Why might too much pleasure or too many rules both cause problems?

- How can something stay balanced while still moving?

- What parts of life need listening instead of control?

- What helps you return when you feel off-balance?

● Learn Like Plato!

A word to notice:

Measure — not as less, but as fitting.

Try this thinking practice:

Notice one part of your day that feels too loud or too quiet.

Ask yourself:

- What is pulling too hard?

- What is being ignored?

- What might stand between them?

You don't need to fix anything.

Just notice where balance might live.

The Walk Continues

The path curved one last time around the garden.

Plato and the scribe walked without hurry now. The stones felt familiar beneath their feet, as if the path itself remembered them.

"You have spoken of the world," the scribe said quietly. "And of time. And of the soul."

Plato nodded.

"And now?" the scribe asked.

Plato slowed, but did not stop. "Now we speak of living."

They passed the olive tree. Theo, Mira, and Leo were still there, though they did not look up this time. They had learned when to listen and when to sit with what they had already heard.

"Living well," Plato said, "is not a matter of choosing the right side."

The scribe wrote.

"It is learning where to stand," Plato continued. "Between too much and too little. Between force and neglect. Between holding on and letting go."

The scribe paused. "The middle again."

Plato smiled. "Always."

They walked on.

"When the soul listens only to desire," Plato said, "life becomes loud and restless. When it listens only to rules, life becomes stiff and narrow."

The scribe nodded. "And when it listens to neither?"

"Then it scatters," Plato replied.

They passed the olive tree once more. The light had shifted, but the tree stood as it always had—uneven, rooted, whole.

"To live in harmony," Plato said, "is not to remove struggle. It is to keep struggle from tearing you apart."

The scribe stopped writing.

"I am writing," he said, "but I don't yet know how to finish."

Plato smiled gently.

"Good. Then you're still living."

They completed the circle.

Plato did not offer a final teaching. He did not turn to face the scribe or the children or the path itself.

He simply kept walking.

And the path, which had never been meant to end, curved onward.

A Last Word to the Reader

Plato never promised answers that would stay still.

He promised that if you walked carefully—returning, listening, and noticing where things belong—you might learn how to hold yourself together in a world that moves.

This is not the end of the walk.

It is only a place to pause.

www.ingramcontent.com/pod-product-compliance
Lightning Source LLC
Chambersburg PA
CBHW081644040426
42449CB00015B/3446